CU00660229

Tour of Longthorpe

Above: The manor house in 1719. The entrance to the medieval hall was through the blocked arched doorway to the right

SETTING

Two miles west of Peterborough city centre, Longthorpe Tower is set back from the high street, 100m west of the parish church, in what until the 1970s was a small village. It contains a vaulted ground-floor room intended for storage, the painted room on the first floor, and a further room above, topped with a battlemented wall-walk. To the west are the other surviving parts of the medieval manor house: the great hall and a two-storey cross-wing, both dating from about 1260. The hall was the largest and most public room in the house, used for dining and entertainment, for manorial business and perhaps for occasionally feeding Robert Thorpe's tenants at certain times of the year. Its main external doorway (partially surviving) faced north (i.e. towards the road) at its extreme west end, and was probably mirrored by a second door directly opposite, forming a 'screens passage' at the west end of the hall. If the normal medieval arrangement was followed, further internal doorways would have led off this passage to service rooms to the west of the hall, from which food and drink were issued, and to a kitchen, all long destroyed.

Above: A 14th-century artist mixing colours

Adjoining the east end of the hall is the two-storey cross-wing, containing, upstairs, the 'great chamber', used both as a place to sleep and as a private reception room. A doorway from the great chamber leads directly into the painted room, at first-floor level, which was yet more private and reserved for honoured guests and clients. Neither the ground floor and wall-walk of the tower, nor the other parts of the house, are open to the public.

FIRST FLOOR OVERVIEW

The painted room was originally only accessible through the door (now locked) from the great chamber. Today the first floor is entered via an outside staircase through a doorway that opens into the painted room. This doorway was created out of a lancet window some time between about 1906 and 1945.

The decoration, covering almost all available surfaces, was painted *a secco*, i.e. onto a dry plastered and lime-washed surface, although some lines were scored in the plaster when wet. The pigments, which include red lead, lead white, chalk and vermilion (brilliant red), were originally much brighter, and some details were gilded. The colours and clarity of the paintings have deteriorated over the centuries since they were made, and much more detail was visible even when they were rediscovered in the 1940s than can be seen today. Our understanding of the scheme relies heavily on records made at that time.

The scheme can be dated by two coats of arms to between 1321 and 1340 and for stylistic reasons to about 1330 (as much as 40 years after the building of the tower). Its realization may conceivably have been prompted either by Thorpe's receipt of knighthood in 1324 or his re-engagement by the abbey in 1330 (see page 19), or both.

The purposes and messages of the scheme, much discussed by historians, would be clearer if more of the abundant French and Latin inscriptions, in elegant Lombardic capitals, had survived. Nevertheless, two main purposes can be identified, the first simply being to create a sumptuous and impressive interior; the second to create a source of immediate delight and entertainment (birds, animals and touches of humour), and viewed more

forensically, of challenge and instruction, through visual, verbal and philosophical riddles, feeding on an interest in numbers (especially twelve, seven, five and three) and their symbolism, inherited from the ancient world. The scheme would also have reminded the viewer of the Thorpes' status and connections, particularly through heraldry and representations of royalty (south wall), and impressed the educated onlooker with the patron's learning. A final, over-arching message was to remind and reassure the onlooker of man's redemption, or deliverance from sin and evil, and the hope of the after-life, granted by the atonement of Jesus Christ, an issue never far from the medieval mind. Thus we have reminders of mortality (the Three Kings and the Ages of Man), and, countering this, the birth of Christ, the Apostles, the Evangelists, a reminder of the way to salvation (St Anthony), and finally allusions to heaven itself, appropriately enough on the ceiling.

Left: A man is dubbed a knight, from an early 14th-century manuscript

EDWARD CLIVE ROUSE'S WATERCOLOURS

When wall-paintings expert E Clive Rouse uncovered and consolidated the Longthorpe paintings in the 1940s, he made, as was his usual practice, a scaled watercolour record of what he found. As the wall

paintings were then brighter and clearer than they are now, Rouse's watercolours often show detail that is hard or impossible to see today. For example, the lettering of the inscription and the details of the

clothes and faces of these two Apostles on the north wall are much clearer in Rouse's drawing (right). For this reason, Rouse's records are used in this guide to illustrate details which are now difficult to see.

Longthorpe's Painters

The elaborate scheme at Longthorpe was the work of professional wall painters familiar with a wide range of contemporary painting and manuscript illustration.

The artists' names are unknown, but differences in style, for example between the head of the king standing behind the Wheel of the Five Senses and that of King David on the ceiling, suggest that there were at least two.

They were aided by assistants, who were responsible for the cruder work, such as the rabbits in the St Anthony scene. The artists were well-paid professionals, and possibly literate, able to avoid the usual errors of mere copyists. Their eclectic style suggests that they were well-travelled and familiar with a wide range of contemporary work, including models preserved in certain manuscripts, such as the Peterborough Psalter, Chronicles and Bestiary (made at the abbey, in about 1299–1321) and the so-called Queen Mary Psalter of about 1310–20. Whether they actually saw such things, or now-lost wall paintings in the same style, is not clear, but certainly they were able to absorb both fashionable and local East Anglian influences from a variety of sources.

Most of the work was done with brushes, and, given the room's height, largely from

wooden staging or scaffolding. The artists or their assistants prepared the paint themselves, in small batches, using a wide and ingenious variety of materials to make the many different colours. The pigments were bound in egg-white, oil or lime, the choice partly depending on the ingredients. The design was set out in rough outline in bold reddish-brown lines, areas of colour and detail then being added in successive layers.

By English and northern European standards the paintings are good – the figures appear in lively stances, the compositions are carefully balanced, and the better faces boldly and successfully drawn. In the broader context of western art, though, they compare less well: at exactly this time, artists of the early Italian Renaissance, led by Giotto di Bondone (1266–1337), were painting with a liveliness, realism and three-dimensionality which would have astonished Thorpe and his painters.

Above: This 13th-century illustration shows an artist sitting on scaffolding to decorate the vault of a room
Left: Detail from the Lamentation *(mourning of Christ) in the Arena Chapel, Padua, Italy, painted by Giotto in about 1305*

View of the west wall

A Labours of the Months   **E** Heraldic banners   **I** St Anthony scene
B Bittern   **F** St Paul   **J** Embroidery style borders
C Crane   **G** St Peter and St Andrew   **K** Pecking bird
D Heraldic shield   **H** Hooded figure   **L** Teaching scene

FIRST FLOOR – WEST WALL

The west wall is largely taken up by a broad, deep recess, housing a lancet window, placed at the extreme north (right-hand) side. The position of this window maximizes the uninterrupted wall surface and is one of several features suggesting that a painted scheme was intended from the start. Above and around the recess are depicted, much damaged, the 'Labours of the Months', a popular medieval theme. The first labour, at lower left, is represented by a man seated at a fire, his cap or hood hanging down his back, holding a bowl of soup; the faint letters

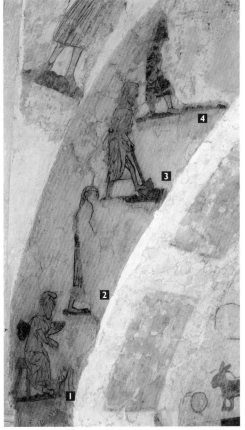

 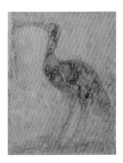

Above: *The crane (right) is similar to this image of the same bird (left) from the Peterborough Bestiary – a medieval treatise describing real and mythical creatures*
Left: *The 'labours' for January, February, March and April*

E CLIVE ROUSE WATERCOLOUR

Above: *Rouse's record drawing of the heraldic banners on the underside of the arch, west wall*

beneath read EANUER, i.e. January **1**. February **2** follows, much damaged, but March **3**, above, is represented by a man digging, preparing for the spring planting, his tunic hitched up for ease of movement. Note the iron edge to his wooden spade. The word APRILIS **4** appears faintly above, but here the figure is mostly missing: in common with other medieval representations of the month, he may have held flowers. Otherwise only December **5**, represented by a man poleaxing a pig, remains legible (lower right).

Beneath January, on the same plane of wall, a bird perches on foliage, pecking. In the equivalent position to the right of the arch is a bittern, and below that a crane. This was based less on life than on conventional medieval depictions, and possibly a particular image in a surviving bestiary (illustrated book of real and mythical creatures) that belonged to Peterborough Abbey.

On the sides and underside of the arch the decoration is largely heraldic. To the south (left), above a small square niche, is a large shield, charged, probably, with the arms of the Watervilles or the d'Eyncourts, local families with whom Thorpe must have had business and perhaps personal connections; above this, and once mirrored by others to the right, appear three square heraldic flags attached to upright poles, the lower one being grasped by a hand (lower right). On the window splays

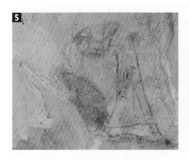 

Left: *This illustration from the Queen Mary Psalter (right), c.1310–20, shows the killing of a pig for Christmas: the usual 'labour' representing the month of December. The equivalent Longthorpe image (left) is now hard to see*

Above: St Paul, holding a sword with his right hand

Above: St Peter (right) and the Prophet Jeremiah (left) from the early 14th-century Peterborough Psalter. The stance of the figures and scrolls are similar to those at Longthorpe, whose artists may have been familiar with this manuscript

appear St Paul (left, with sword in scabbard), while St Peter (holding keys) and St Andrew holding a saltire (drawn with single red lines) face each other on the right. These form the first in a series, originally of 13 figures, mostly representing the Apostles, which continues across the north wall (see pages 9–10). In the alcove to the right of the window, a hooded figure addresses a child, holding a scroll reading 'NO[TR]E DAME N[O]US ASOUDRA DE LA PE[CHE]', i.e. 'Our Lady will absolve us from sin'.

E CLIVE ROUSE WATERCOLOUR

Above: Rouse's record (right) of the scene in the alcove to the right of the window shows detail of the inscription and figures which is now almost impossible to see (left)

Above: St Anthony (left) receives advice from God, whose head and shoulders, Rouse observed, were shown appearing above

The main wall surface, at the back of the recess, carries two scenes. At the top, a man stands praying (left), and opposite another sits making a basket, with a further figure standing behind him, while, although not legible today, God (originally represented by head and shoulders) watched from above. This otherwise puzzling subject is identified by the part-surviving inscription, taken from a life of St Anthony, in which he asks God how to find salvation, and in answer is confronted by an angel alternately working (making a basket) and praying (the figure behind), and advising 'Do thus and you will be saved' (see the last fragments of the inscription: [SIC FAC ET S]ALVUS ER[IS]). St Anthony's status as patron saint of basket-makers, and perhaps also its renown as a fenland craft, explains the choice of trade to illustrate 'work'. Behind the saint, two naïvely drawn rabbits and four birds perched on a pair of trees denote the wilderness setting.

Below this scene is a broad border, probably imitating an embroidered textile, bearing depictions (left to right) of a lapwing, an owl and a bestiary-derived parrot. Further birds appear on the vertical left-hand border. Framed by the border are two men with a tree between them, one seated and probably teaching, and the other standing. The scene is perhaps unfinished.

E CLIVE ROUSE WATERCOLOUR

Above: Detail from Rouse's record. The basket-maker, seated on a stuffed sack, uses a mallet to press down the weavers (the horizontal withies)

View of the north wall

A The Nativity   **C** Apostles   **E** Ostriches and storks
B Seven Ages of Man   **D** 'Holy Catholic Church'   **F** Heraldry

FIRST FLOOR – NORTH WALL

The north wall originally framed a broad recess, as on the west, but was thickened in about 1320 in an attempt to counteract minor subsidence (see the cracks on the exterior), creating the existing window embrasure. The mullions are of about 1600. Above the window the central scene depicts the Nativity: the Virgin reclines on a boarded chair to the left, feeding the swaddled Christ, with Joseph seated on a post and rail chair to the right. Above the damaged central area, originally showing the crib, can be seen the ears of the ass, and a horn and ear of the ox. Above and around all this, separated by a dark red band with written labels, are depicted the 'Seven Ages of Man', a popular theme since antiquity. The message is reinforced by the ascent of

successive images around the arch from infancy to prime, and the symmetrical descent to decrepitude on the other side. Much detail is missing, but the figures and parts of the accompanying Latin labels remain legible: starting with the cradled infant at lower left (INFANS) **1**, representations follow of boyhood (with whip and spinning top), adolescence (damaged), youth (with hawk) **2**, manhood (sword) old age (life savings), and decrepitude (DECREPITUS, with crutch) **3**.

Below, to the left of the window embrasure, two standing figures continue the series of Apostles begun on the west wall, which then carries on across both splays of the north window embrasure (originally two figures to each splay), the wall to the right of the window embrasure, and then onto the left-hand splay of what is now the entrance

Above: Nativity scene from the Queen Mary Psalter displaying a similar composition to the Longthorpe scene (top) and showing the manger, the ox and the ass which Longthorpe now lacks

Below: Details from the Seven Ages of Man sequence

Above: Female figure representing the Church (left), with the Apostle Thaddaeus to the right

doorway. Beginning as was customary with St Paul (not an Apostle), the series of 12 further figures is ordered as in the early medieval Canon of the Mass, and each originally held a scroll bearing the article of the Apostles' Creed which he was believed to have contributed. An odd one out on this wall is the female figure (hooded, veiled and haloed, immediately to the right of the window embrasure), in place of James the Less, but her allocated text, beginning [SANCTAM] ECCLESIAM CATHOLICAM, i.e. 'the Holy Catholic Church', the ninth article of the Creed, suggests that she represents the Church (*Ecclesia*) as an institution.

Four large birds fill the lowest register of decoration – bestiary-derived ostriches at the extreme ends and stork-like specimens at either side of the window embrasure.

On the ceiling of the embrasure are the remains of four shields, one of which (on the right, with each quarter *gyronny*, i.e. split diagonally), is the coat of the Bassingbourns, a local family.

Below: The ostrich (left) may have been based on this depiction of ostriches (right) in the 14th-century Peterborough Bestiary

View of the east wall

A Apostles

B Bearded man with pupils

C Remains of lancet window

D Three Living and the Three Dead

E Wheel of the Five Senses

F Upper scene

FIRST FLOOR – EAST WALL

The left splay of the doorway embrasure displays the last two in the series of Apostles – Simon and then Matthias, who took the place of Judas Iscariot. In the niche below, a bearded older man is seen addressing three young ones. Above the doorway to the left can be seen the surround of the original lancet window (re-exposed in the 1940s), and to the right of this, carried on above the adjacent doorway to the latrine, a representation of the 'Three Living Kings and the Three Dead Kings' – a variation of a well-known medieval memento of mortality, loosely based on a 13th-century poem. The first of the living kings, originally over the doorway, is missing, but the second can be identified by his prominent red

E CLIVE ROUSE WATERCOLOUR

Above: A bearded man addresses three pupils. On the scroll, Rouse made out the word OREILLE[Z], probably meaning 'hear me' in Old French

The Three Living and the Three Dead

The scene shows the living kings admonishing the dead ones for startling them. The spectres then identify themselves as the kings' forebears and rebuke them for failing to say masses for their souls. The story may first have been told by the Flemish poet Baudouin de Condé in the 13th century, and became a popular theme in medieval art and literature. Its moral message relates to the transitory nature of man's earthly existence.

crown, while the third is speaking, finger raised, to the first of the dead kings. He and his neighbour wear tattered shrouds – originally white and now black (the original white lead carbonate in the pigment has turned to black lead dioxide) – but the third dead king is naked and crawls with maggots (now also black).

The principal scene on the main surface of the east wall shows a standing figure, a large wheel, and a number of creatures. This is essentially a conflation of the graphic concept of the 'Wheel of Fortune' or 'Wheel of Life' and the literary pairing of animals and senses, ultimately derived from Aristotle and Pliny, but formalized in the mid 13th-century *Liber de Naturis Rerum* (*Book of the Nature of Things*) by the Flemish Dominican friar Thomas de Cantimpré. Historians have called it the 'Wheel of the Five Senses'. Around the rim, clockwise from lower left, are depicted a monkey (eating, representing taste), a hawk (smell), a spider's web (touch), a poorly drawn mammal, and the head of a cockerel (sight). If Cantimpré was the model, the mammal is

meant to be a boar (hearing) and the hawk a vulture (the artist probably never having seen a vulture, he drew his best approximation). The figure standing behind the wheel holds a spoke with one hand and points to the rim with the other, perhaps indicating control and understanding. Inscriptions on the rim and spokes, now illegible, would have made the meaning clear. The point, however, was probably to contrast the inferiority of man's senses with his unique possession of reason, and the resulting ability and obligation to

Right: The closest known parallel to the Longthorpe 'wheel', in a house at Constance, south Germany, c.1320, and clearly based on Cantimpré. The five creatures are linked by lines to the enthroned king. The boar and vulture can be clearly seen to the left

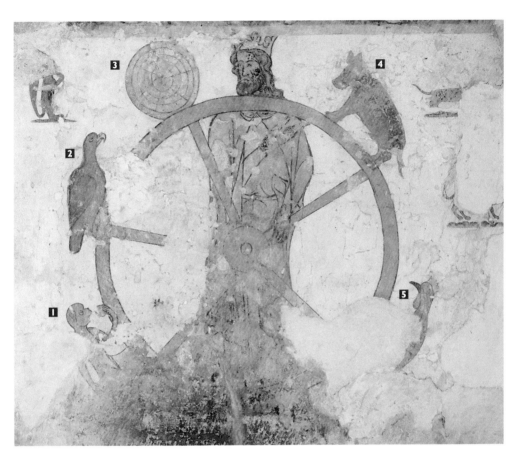

Above: The Wheel of the Five Senses

1 Monkey (taste)
2 Hawk (smell)
3 Spider's web (touch)
4 Boar (hearing)
5 Cockerel (sight)

Left: The cockerel, showing faint traces of the painter's first attempt above it

represented by animals, are connected by lines to the relevant features of a crowned seated figure.

To the right of the main scene are two hounds, much damaged but markedly different, while at the top left a squirrel (missing the head) sits up, eating.

The large scene above shows the standing figure of a young man, holding his gloves, with a dog standing behind. He is in animated conversation with the figure to the left, of whom little more than the right foot, scabbard and raised index finger survive. Originally, the meaning of scene would have been explained by the long inscription between the figures, now indecipherable.

control impulses triggered by sensory experience: the fact that the man is crowned may allude to the particular importance of such restraint by those in power. More elaborate interpretations derived from Aristotelian philosophy, however, abound.

Whatever its precise meaning, the composition is of extreme rarity, only two parallels being known: one a 13th-century example in the Cistercian monastery of Tre Fontane in Rome; the other a domestic wall painting of similar date at Constance (south-west Germany), in which the senses,

Right: An elegant young man from the upper east wall, who stands holding his gloves

View of the south wall

A Imitation cloth hanging
B Arms of King Edward III
C King Edward III
D Arms of Edmund of Woodstock
E Edmund of Woodstock
F Bonnacon
G Door to great chamber (not accessible)
H Door to second floor

Above: An imposing chair raised on a dais, depicted in a French manuscript of about 1400. Thorpe may have used something very similar, placed against the south wall

FIRST FLOOR – SOUTH WALL

The lower register of the south wall is painted to mimic a cloth hanging, a common medieval device, on which a variant of the Thorpe arms, identifiable by the horizontal band (*fess*) and the six stylized lilies (*fleurs de lis*), alternate with another, now unreadable. The *fleurs de lis*, originally white or gold, but now represented by the red underpainting, can best be seen at the top left. Above sit two enthroned figures flanked by shields, the one to the left bearing the royal arms of England as used until 1340 (after which it was quartered with *fleurs de lis*), and who may represent Edward II (r.1307–26) or more probably Edward III (r.1326–77). The other shield, bearing (according to Rouse's

E CLIVE ROUSE WATERCOLOUR

Above: Rouse's record of the royal coat of arms (left), which probably identifies the left-hand seated figure as Edward III. Today (right), the lions on the shield are difficult to make out

observations in the 1940s) the same three lions passant gardant (i.e. lions or leopards walking with heads facing the viewer), but with a still visible white border, identifies the right-hand figure as Edmund of Woodstock, Earl of Kent, half-brother of Edward II, judicially murdered in 1330. The reasons for their presence here have been much discussed, but the simplest and most convincing explanation is that it pays homage to the king as Robert Thorpe's employer (or former employer) and to the earl perhaps as a landlord; it would in any case have drawn attention to Thorpe's strong links with the ruling elite.

Real and fictive hangings such as the one here – once rich with colour, gold and heraldry – were common backdrops for throne-like chairs, and it may have been from here, seated close to the fireplace with the great dynastic mural overhead, that Thorpe received his guests and clients.

To the lower right, over the doorways, an archer (the figure is missing) rashly aims at the back end of a bonnacon, a mythological beast

which showered assailants with flaming excrement. Its inclusion may just be for fun, or, conceivably, may convey some sort of political or satirical message.

Above: The bonnacon, as depicted at Longthorpe (top) and in the Peterborough Bestiary (below)

View of the ceiling

A Bagpiper
B Eagle of St John
C King David

D Psaltery player
E Figures lost – possibly *cymbalum* players

F Organ player
G Ox of St Luke
H Rebec players

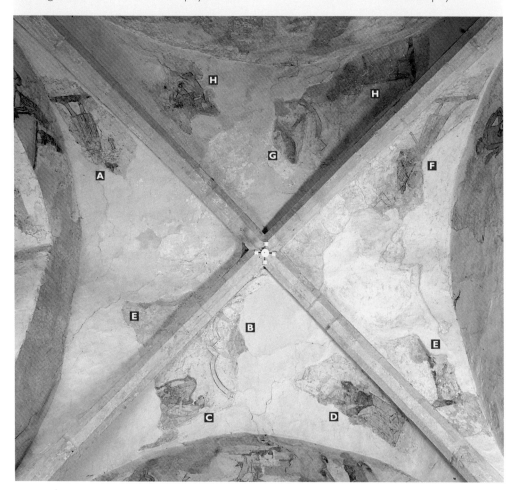

Below: Bagpipers, as depicted at Longthorpe (left) and in the near-contemporary Luttrell Psalter (right), representing the 'trumpet' (tuba) of Psalm 150

FIRST FLOOR – CEILING

Each of the vault's four quarters displayed one of the symbols of the four Evangelists (the authors of the four Gospels), and musical instruments being played, with one exception, by angels. The musicians illustrate the words of Psalm 150 ('Praise him with the sound of the trumpet …') and all but one of the seven instruments it names can be identified. The intent was partly to represent heaven, held to be filled with music and, as the ultimate destination of the saved, to underline the scheme's overall reference to redemption and salvation.

In the west quarter (above the St Anthony scene) the Evangelist's symbol is missing, but

Above: King David plays the harp. At first the artist placed the hands too low down, then repainted them higher up. The mistake has since re-emerged through his over-painting

Above: Psaltery players, as depicted at Longthorpe (left) and in the 14th-century Queen Mary Psalter (right)

must have been the lion of St Mark or the angel of St Matthew. To the left, an angel plays a bagpipe, representing the 'trumpet' of the psalm; to the right an angel played, presumably, a stringed instrument or the *cymbalum* (a row of bells). In the north quarter, the eagle of St John, labelled JOHANNES, is flanked by King David (left) – known from the Old Testament as a musician and in medieval lore as a harpist – and on the right a psaltery player. On the east quarter the symbol (a lion or angel) is lost, but to the right an angel plays a 16-pipe portative organ. The figure opposite, of which only the lower legs survive, could also have been a string or *cymbalum* player. Finally, the south quarter displays the ox of St Luke and angels playing the rebec, a precursor of the viol and violin, and (just visible to the right) the upper rim of a drum.

Left: A cymbalum *player from the 13th-century Peterborough Psalter sits by his instrument, a row of bells suspended from a bar*
Below: Portative organs: the Longthorpe player on the left and from the Luttrell Psalter on the right

Below: Musicians playing the rebec, an ancestor of the viol and violin, in depictions at Longthorpe (left and middle) and in the 14th-century Queen Mary Psalter (right)

SECOND FLOOR

The second-floor room seems not to have been painted, but remains a remarkably complete 14th-century domestic interior. It has single-light windows on all sides, all with 'shouldered' heads, three of which retain the slot for a draw-bar to fasten internal shutters. Doors opening from the sides of the southern window embrasure lead to a latrine (left), originally projecting from the exterior, and (right) to a stair to the parapet walk overhead (not accessible to visitors). The exposed roof-carpentry, re-set in the 1940s, is of pyramidal form, and retains a central moulded strut, four-way collars and other timbers which probably date from the 15th century. The original roof may have been flat. The presence of a latrine but the absence of a fireplace suggest that this was a bedroom. A turret at the head of the stair opens onto the narrow, leaded parapet walk. The parapet and the loopholed battlements at the corners, probably designed to mimic the corner turrets of a great tower of the 11th or 12th century, are original. The octagonal medieval chimney-stack also partly survives.

Above: The tower's second-floor room. The narrow doorway in the recess to the right leads to a latrine

Below: The original parapet, corner battlement and octagonal medieval chimney

Below: Historic photograph taken from the parapet, looking south-west, when the manor was still a working farm. The roof of the manor's great hall can be seen in the foreground, below. The medieval service buildings would have stood beyond, where the farm buildings are located. A 17th-century square dovecote stands to the left

History of Longthorpe Tower

THE MANOR OF LONGTHORPE

The first known member of the family who built and occupied the house and tower is a William of Thorpe, mentioned in 1174–5 and dead by 1199. His son Thurstan held lands in the manor of Longthorpe from the Watervilles of nearby Orton Waterville, and of Peterborough Abbey. By 1219 Thurstan's son William (II) had succeeded, and in about 1250–70 built the surviving hall and 'great chamber', probably replacing an earlier house on the same site. Between 1263 and 1274 he paid to replace the distant parochial chapel – now long destroyed – with the existing building, ostensibly for the convenience of the parishioners, but also to add lustre to the surroundings and standing of his house. His heir, William (III), succeeded by the mid 1270s, and died in 1294.

Top: The tower from the east, showing the existing entrance, created by enlarging a medieval window
Above: Illumination of about 1325–50 showing a lawyer seated with a group of monks

ROBERT THORPE

William's son Robert (Robert I) was responsible for building the tower and its painted interior. Robert first appears in documents in 1293, as a lawyer, the profession by which he and his family rose to prominence in the following century, and by 1300 was regularly acting for Peterborough Abbey. In 1309 he became the abbey's lay steward, responsible for upholding the abbey's rights in the 'Liberty' or 'Soke' of Peterborough (the vast area around the town under its jurisdiction) and its chief legal officer, aided by a substantial staff. While this appointment enhanced his social position, it remained an unusual one, although by then shared by a small and rising class of lawyers in similar positions elsewhere: he was both a major tenant and employee of the abbey, a professional man, occupant of a powerful office, owner of a fine house, growing richer off legal fees, perks of office and landed income, but not yet a knight and socially inferior to the knightly class. By 1317 Robert I had left his post as steward and was working for the king, and by 1320 had taken knighthood. In 1330, however, he was re-appointed as steward. He died in or soon after 1354.

Above: *Reconstructed overview* **1** Tower   **3** Great hall   **5** Detached kitchen
of the manor in the 1330s   **2** Great chamber wing   **4** Service wing   **6** Additional service buildings

BUILDING THE TOWER

People had been attaching towers to grand but otherwise ordinary houses since at least the 12th century and the practice outlasted the Middle Ages. In most cases they contained additional private rooms, and are sometimes called 'solar towers'. But this was a costly way of adding extra space, and most were also intended, in varying proportions, to provide security and as status symbols, drawing on the associations of towers with authority, martial prowess and ancient lineage. In Thorpe's case, given his social position, it was probably its symbolic potential that led him, between about 1290 and 1300, to add the 12m (40-foot) stone tower to his home. Nevertheless, it also housed a special room and, in an area then frequented by marauding gangs and bandits, promised some security (if, as it proved, illusory: see page 22) for his family, valuables and documents.

Solar Towers

'Solar' is a medieval word of Latin origin, but usually described a bedchamber, generally at an upper level.

From the late pre-Conquest period until the late 16th century, rich men sometimes enhanced their houses with a tower containing one or more rooms, usually one above the other, to create what are now termed 'solar towers'. These provided extra private space and sometimes security, but their main purpose was as status symbols, drawing on contemporary connotations of towers and battlements with martial valour and ancient lineage. Sometimes, as in the case of Longthorpe and, for example, Stokesay Castle, Shropshire (built about 1280), their building was clearly

prompted by the contrast between their owners' lowly origins and their social aspirations.

The best-known 'solar towers', many genuinely defensible, are among the so-called 'pele towers' built on both sides of the Scottish border between about 1350 and 1500. Closer analogies to Longthorpe include Little Wenham Hall, Suffolk, built about 1265–80, and once also attached to a ground-floor hall.

Left: *Late 13th-century solar tower at Little Wenham, Suffolk*

Architecturally the tower is interesting in that its unornamented, four-square form, and the corner-turret outline of its battlements, suggest a direct evocation of the great Romanesque towers of the 12th century, such as at Hedingham (Essex), rather than their more domesticated derivatives such as Stokesay Castle (Shropshire, c.1280), or the more local example at Little Wenham (Suffolk, c.1265–80). For a 'solar tower', it is also extremely early, as most surviving examples date from the late 14th or 15th century.

THE PAINTED ROOM

The design of the room, in particular the placing of the windows to leave broad, uninterrupted wall surfaces, suggests that an ambitious decorative scheme was intended from the start. The existing decoration is dated to between 1321 and 1340 by two coats of arms, and for stylistic reasons to about 1330. The combination of the room's small size, lavish decoration, and accessibility only through the main bedchamber of the house suggests this was a private place to receive honoured guests and clients, to relax, to work, and to contemplate. This is in keeping with the painted subject-matter, which would have impressed the viewer with its patron's devotion, learning, wealth, grand connections and links with royalty. Thorpe himself, meanwhile, would have been reassured by comforting symbols of his status (including his own coat of arms) but also reminded of his own mortality. Learned, Latin-literate and with access to Peterborough Abbey's famous library, Thorpe probably chose these themes himself. The concentration on erudition, rather than the chivalric and martial scenes beloved of the purely knightly class, reflects the nature and values of Robert's profession.

Connections with the abbey, an important artistic patron, probably also helped him commission sophisticated painters. Quite how exceptional such a concentration of figurative painting may have been in 14th-century houses is unknown, but the presence of this scheme in a relatively modest building hints that they were more common than might otherwise be

E CLIVE ROUSE WATERCOLOUR

Above: Rouse's record of the eagle, painted in a roundel and surrounded by false-ashlaring, found on the inner gable wall of the manor house's great chamber

suggested. Of the other rooms at Longthorpe, only the great chamber is known to have been painted, thanks to the survival of an area of false-ashlaring (lines imitating cut stone) and a much damaged eagle (the symbol of St John) on the inside of the north gable. The hall may also have had painted decoration; the tower's upper chamber did not.

Below: This 13th-century illumination shows an artist working from a portable scaffold, with his pots of paint at his feet

THE LATER THORPES AND THEIR SUCCESSORS

Two generations of Robert I's descendants held Longthorpe until the death of his grandson, William V, in 1391, although from the 1350s their principal house was at Maxey (Cambridgeshire) ten miles north-west. Robert I's sons, Robert II and William IV, were both distinguished lawyers, William (d.1361) becoming Chief Justice of the King's Bench in 1346, and Robert (d.1372) Chancellor of England in 1371. Both did much to enrich the family and William's grant of the 'freedom to crenellate' or fortify Maxey, swiftly acted on, marked the family's rise from the upper gentry to quasi-noble status. William's heir, William V,

died childless in 1391, leaving Longthorpe to his relative John Whittlebury, formerly an MP for Rutland.

The Whittleburys were based in Whissendine (Rutland), and Longthorpe remained a secondary residence or let to tenants. In 1502 it seems to have

Right: A depiction of the now-lost tomb of Robert Thorpe II in Peterborough Abbey from William Dugdale's Book of Monuments, 1640–41

Burglary and Ransom

On 10 December 1327, three judges were authorized to hear and determine a case brought by Robert Thorpe against Richard, Roger and Robert of Whatton, Walter Warde of Ufford, Hugh of Badyngton and Thomas atte Noke of Upton. These men, Thorpe claimed, had 'together with other wrongdoers and disturbers of the peace by force of arms broken [into] his houses and chests at Benefield and Thorpe', stealing £200 worth of goods, and had 'imprisoned, detained and mistreated' him until Thorpe promised to pay £100 in ransom. Thorpe's house at Benefield, a secondary residence near Oundle, may have been an easier target, but despite its appearance of security, Longthorpe's stone tower clearly failed to protect Thorpe and his goods from the thieves.

Above: A man offering a ransom, about 1325. Robbers forced Robert Thorpe to pay them £100

Thorpe was a victim of a rash of violence in the early years of Edward III's reign, particularly endemic in the Midlands. The most serious perpetrators were gangs supported by vagrant criminals (the 'other wrongdoers') but often led by men of property, shielded from the law by other gentry and clergy: this was the milieu, and probably the

period, which spawned the legends of Robin Hood. Their crimes – burglary and highway robbery apart – included kidnapping, blackmail and extortion; their motivation was primarily gain, but also revenge, and Thorpe was not the first legal man to be so treated. Thorpe may have exaggerated his losses, but the size of the ransom and the value of the stolen goods are colossal – a testament if nothing else to Thorpe's wealth.

Above: 15th-century manuscript illustration of armed men carrying off household goods

been bought by a London merchant, William Fitzwilliam. Some confusion remains as to which of the several manors in Thorpe were held, over the next 450 years, by the Fitzwilliam family and which by the abbey and its heirs, the Dean and Chapter of Peterborough. While some attempt had been made in the Middle Ages to repaint damaged areas of painting, others were later deliberately defaced. Later still, whether for reasons of taste or post-Reformation ideology, the whole scheme was whitewashed.

Above: A watercolour of about 1910 showing the interior of the painted room with the decoration still concealed

ANTIQUARIAN INTEREST AND DISCOVERY

The first known antiquarian interest in the tower was that of John Bridges (1666–1724), who was compiling material for his projected history of Northamptonshire, eventually published in 1791. He visited Longthorpe in 1718, 1719 and 1721, on the second occasion accompanied by his Flemish draughtsman Peter Tillemans (1684–1734). The first description of the building, albeit brief, appears in Thomas Hudson Turner's *Some Account of Domestic Architecture* of 1852, accompanied by an engraving based on a drawing by Edward Blore (1787–1879). JH Parker, Hudson Turner's continuator, took members of the Royal Archaeological Institute there in 1861, and published an article in the *Gentleman's Magazine* a year later. *The Victoria County History* of 1906 included a partial plan of the buildings and JA Gotch published a derivative in 1936. But real interest in the site began with the discovery of the paintings in 1945 by the tenant, Hugh Horrell, under layers of whitewash and more recent distemper, while preparing to redecorate the interiors after use by the Home Guard. Horrell reported the find to the owner, Captain WTG Fitzwilliam (later 10th Earl Fitzwilliam), and his agent, Herbert Elliot, who sought the advice of the Society of Antiquaries of London.

Below: Longthorpe manor from the north-west, drawn about 1850 by the architect and antiquarian Edward Blore

CONSERVATION AND THE FUTURE

On the Society's advice, the estate called in their Fellow, Edward Clive Rouse (1901–97), pupil of the pioneering wall-painting specialist Ernest William Tristram (1882–1952), to advise. Rouse then spent 'many months' in 1946–8 uncovering, consolidating and making a drawn record of the paintings. Importantly, he made no attempt to restore or 'touch up' the paintings, leaving the colours – some drastically altered over time by chemical action – as he found them. Unfortunately, the removal of the limewash took with it much of the original surface, losing much of the subtlety of the original finish. In addition, as was the practice of the time, Rouse used wax as a consolidant, inadvertently sealing moisture behind the paint and causing further damage, so that in the 1980s most of the treatment had to be removed. Regular monitoring since has shown the paintings, although inherently fragile, to be in remarkably stable condition. In the future, use of techniques not available to Rouse may allow further details to be revealed and for the paintings to be more permanently protected.

Captain Fitzwilliam gave Longthorpe Tower to the nation in 1948, to be cared for by the Ministry of Works and from 1984 by English Heritage. Since 2012 it has been managed by Vivacity Culture and Leisure, a local not-for-profit organization with charitable status.

'The room is overwhelmingly impressive and it is impossible not to be amazed at the richness of the decoration' (E Clive Rouse, 1955). This photograph shows Rouse undertaking restoration of the paintings in the late 1940s.

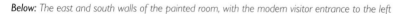

Below: The east and south walls of the painted room, with the modern visitor entrance to the left